RIVER ADVENTURES
AMAZON RIVER

A+

Smart Apple Media

Published by Smart Apple Media
P.O. Box 3263, Mankato, Minnesota 56002
www.smartapplemedia.com

Published by arrangement with the Watts Publishing
Group LTD, London.

Designed, edited and produced by Paul Manning
Maps by Stefan Chabluk

Library of Congress Cataloging-in-Publication Data

Manning, Paul.
 Amazon River / Paul Manning.
    p. cm. -- (River adventures)
 Summary: "Readers will journey down the amazing
Amazon River in this exciting adventure. Beginning in
Peru, readers will learn about ancient civilizations and
exotic animals, as well as modern people and cities on
the Amazon River"--Provided by publisher.
 Includes bibliographical references and index.
 ISBN 978-1-59920-914-2
 1. Amazon River--Juvenile literature. I. Title.
 F2546.M324 2015
 981'.1--dc23
                                        2012026573

 ISBN: 978-1-59920-914-2   (library binding)
 ISBN: 978-1-62588-584-5   (eBook)

Printed in the United States by CG Book Printers
North Mankato, Minnesota

PO 1732
3-2015

9 8 7 6 5 4 3 2 1

Note to Teachers and Parents

Key to images

Top cover image: Dense Amazon rain forest
Main cover image: A steamer on the Amazon river
Previous page: An Amazon river dolphin
This page: The Amazon floodplain during the
rainy season.

Picture Credits

Contents

An Amazon Journey

The Amazon River stretches for 4,250 miles (6,840 km). It is the second longest river in the world. Thousands of animal **species** live in the river, from piranha fish to pink river dolphins. You will follow the river from its source high in the Andes Mountains to its mouth on the eastern coast of Brazil.

A Mighty River

The Amazon is so vast that it often seems more like a sea than a river. Its width varies from 1 to 6.2 miles (1.6 to 10 km). In the rainy season, some places widen to more than 30 miles (48 km) across. On its journey, it is joined by hundreds of other rivers called **tributaries**. Where the Amazon enters the Atlantic Ocean, its **estuary** measures 149 miles (240 km) across—nearly the same width as Lake Superior.

The Amazon Basin

The area drained by the river is called the Amazon basin. This covers about 40 percent of South America. The Amazon basin is covered by tropical rain forest. This forest is one of the richest sources of plant and animal life on Earth.

▲ Together with its tributaries, the Amazon carries more water than any river in the world.

▼ The jaguar is one of millions of animal species found in the Amazon rainforest.

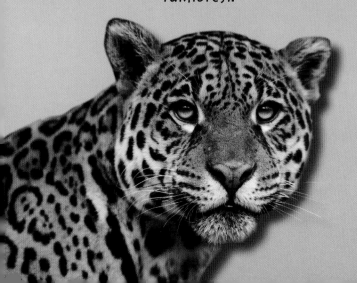

Naming the Amazon

The first European to explore the Amazon was Francisco de Orellana, a Spanish soldier, in the 1540s. Returning from his adventures, Orellana told of fighting with fierce women warriors who lived in the Brazilian jungle. The Spanish king Charles V later named the river Amazonas after the women warriors of Greek mythology.

5

The High Andes

YOU ARE HERE

Your river adventure starts high in the Andes Mountains of Peru. Here, the Amazon is fed by many different rivers called **headwaters**.

The Amazon's Source

The Amazon's source is a tiny stream on a volcanic mountain peak called Nevado Mismi. At the foot of a cliff, a simple wooden cross marks the spot where the river begins. Swollen by rain and melted snow, the stream turns into a fast-flowing river. Eventually, it joins the Apurímac River. This joins other rivers that feed into the Amazon farther north.

◀ A scientific expedition in 2001 confirmed this spot as the source of the Amazon river.

◀ The city of Machu Picchu is one of the most important surviving relics of the Inca empire.

An Inca Stronghold

The Inca rulers who built Machu Picchu chose the site well. The city is surrounded on three sides by the Urubamba River, a tributary of the Amazon. It is perched on cliffs that rise 1,476 feet (450 m). The city's location was a closely guarded secret, and the mountains and river around it made it a natural fortress.

The Incas

Centuries ago, the valleys of Amazon tributaries such as the Apurímac and the Urubamba gave food and shelter to people called Incas. The Incas built a great civilization that spread throughout the region. In the 1500s, the Incas were conquered by Spanish soldiers, but many traces of their cities and culture remain.

The most famous Inca site is the city of Machu Picchu. In the 1400s, it was the home of the Inca rulers, but was abandoned when the Spanish invaded. In 1911, it was rediscovered by a visiting American historian. Today, it is one of South America's most important historic sites.

▼ Inca craftsmen were skilled metalworkers. This ceremonial mask is made of copper.

Farming the Andes

BRAZIL

Urubamba River

PERU

Apurimac River

Lima

Machu Picchu

ANDES MOUNTAINS

Pacific Ocean

YOU ARE HERE

In the high Andes valleys, you meet the local people who farm the land. They are known as the Quechua. Many of them are descended from the Incas who once lived here.

▼ This valley was carved by the Urubamba River, a tributary of the Amazon. It was **sacred** to the Incas because of the fish, water, and other resources it provided.

Crop Rotation

The Quechua farm the land in the same way as the Incas before them. They grow different crops side by side, and vary them from year to year to allow the soil to recover. They also raise herds of llama and alpaca. They use the wool to make warm clothes to wear in the winter.

◀ Terraces allow crops such as corn to be grown on the sloping valley sides.

Life in the Valleys

In **prehistoric** times, the high Andes valleys were among the earliest places to be inhabited by humans. The valleys gave shelter from the wind and sun, creating cooler temperatures in the daytime and warmer temperatures at night. Civilizations grew from these river valley communities.

Terraces

On the valley floor, every patch of land is used for growing. On the hillsides, the Quechua farmers have created strips of level land called **terraces**, so that they can plant more crops. These are supplied with water from the river by channels carved in the rock.

The climate is harsh in the mountains, and it is hard to make a living by farming. Because of this, some Quechuas are beginning to leave the area and move to towns farther down the valley.

▶ A traditionally dressed Quechua girl with her alpaca

YOU ARE HERE

Amazon Lowlands

Heading north, you leave the mountains and enter the lowlands of eastern Peru. At Nauta, the rivers Ucayali and Marañón meet, and the main Amazon River begins.

Tropical Rain Forest

This area is close to the Equator, and the air is hot and sticky. Dense jungle stretches as far as the eye can see. Overhead, the trees form a roof called a **canopy**. In places, the canopy is so thick that sunlight hardly reaches the ground. This landscape is called tropical rain forest.

It rains here year round, and moisture drips constantly from the leaves and branches. The rain swells the river, adding to the flow from the mountains farther south.

◀ In the rain forest, tall trees are supported by spreading roots that reach down to collect **nutrients** from the soil.

Amerindians

People called Amerindians have lived in this region for thousands of years. When Europeans first explored the Amazon basin in the 1500s, about 2 million Amerindians lived here. Today, barely 250,000 are left. Some were killed by foreign invaders. Others were forced to work as **slaves** on **plantations**. Many died of diseases brought by European settlers.

Today, the biggest threat to Amerindians is the loss of their land through mining, road building, cattle ranching, and **logging**. Some now live in reservations where they live traditionally and pass on their culture to their children.

▲ These Amerindian children belong to a tribe called the Asháninka.

The Yagua

Yagua people originally came from Peru. They now live in about 30 villages scattered throughout the Peruvian and Colombian Amazon basin. The Yagua live by farming, fishing, and hunting. They are skilled at carving animal figures from wood, bone, and other materials.

◄ A Yagua tribal elder shows his skill with the **blowgun**, a weapon used for hunting.

Iquitos

About 62 miles (100 km) from Nauta, you reach the city of Iquitos. More than 400,000 people live here. It is the largest city in the world that cannot be reached by roads.

At the riverside, you watch boats unloading cargo. The river is a lifeline for Iquitos, and the port and riverside markets are always busy. From Iquitos, goods are shipped along the Amazon to other towns near and far. This river trade is vital to the city.

YOU ARE HERE

▼ Local traders unload a cargo of bananas to sell at the Iquitos market. Fish, fruits and vegetables, tobacco, and timber are also traded here.

▲ In the rainy season, the Amazon can rise by up to 30 feet (9 m). These homes in Iquitos are built on **stilts** and floating rafts of balsa wood. This protects them from being flooded.

▼ A rubber tapper collects latex, the milky white sap that is used to make rubber.

Natural Resources

The land around Iquitos is rich in timber and other **natural resources**. Natural rubber is collected from the trees in the forest. There are also stocks of oil and gas under the ground. These are sold to other countries, including the United States.

The oil industry has brought money and jobs to the region, but it has also brought pollution. In October 2000, about 5,500 barrels of oil spilled into the Marañón river. Fish died, and many people became sick from drinking **contaminated** water.

Natural Rubber

In the past, the rubber trade brought vast wealth to the cities of the Amazon. Thousands of Amerindians worked as slaves collecting rubber from trees in the forest. "Rubber barons" made huge fortunes from slave labor. The boom ended with cheap foreign competition, but the rubber industry still continues in the Amazon region.

The Rio Solimões

YOU ARE HERE

At the town of Leticia, you cross the border from Peru into Brazil. Here, the Amazon is known as the Rio Solimões. Much of Brazil's vast rain forest region has never been explored.

▼ Thick rain forest lines the banks of the Brazilian Amazon.

Navigating the River

Traveling through the rain forest by road is very difficult, so the river is a vital transportation route. From time to time, you pass local traders using small boats and **dugout canoes** to take their goods to market. You also see rafts and barges transporting heavier goods, such as timber, out of the forest.

◀ In its middle course, the Amazon flows in giant loops called meanders.

Meanders

A **meander** is formed when a river washes away stones and mud on the outside of a bend and drops it on the opposite bank. Over time, this gradually causes the bend to widen. Sometimes, the bend becomes so wide that the river joins up with itself. When this happens, a horseshoe-shaped "oxbow lake" is formed, away from the main river.

River Creatures

As you make your way downriver, your guide points out a pair of manatees in the water. These gentle, seal-like creatures can grow up to 10 feet (3 m) long, but are shy and rarely seen. The river is also home to turtles, alligators, lizards, river dolphins, and thousands of fish species, from giant pirarucu to flesh-eating piranhas.

▶ Manatees are sometimes known as sea cows. They are usually found in shallow, slow-moving waters.

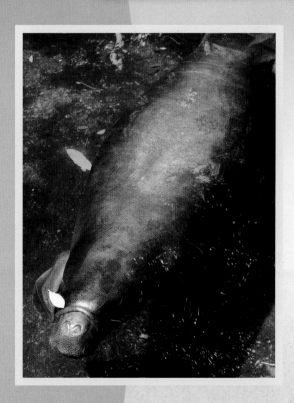

Life on the River

YOU ARE HERE

Deep in the rain forest, you pass a remote village by the river. These people are far away from any towns. They rely on the river and the land around them for food and shelter.

▶ Fish from the river are a vital food for people living by the Amazon.

Hunting and Gathering

In the past, the rain forest was inhabited by Amerindian tribes who lived entirely by hunting and gathering. The Amerindians caught fish from the river and boiled it in pots or smoked it over a fire to preserve it. Animals were hunted with bows and arrows or killed with darts tipped with a poison found in the rain forest. Only a few Amerindians still live this way.

◄ Amerindian children enjoy a meal of freshly caught fish cooked over a wood fire.

Subsistence Farming

Today, most of the people who occupy forest land are **subsistence farmers**. They grow crops like manioc and rice on small plots of land, producing just enough to feed their families. After a time, the heavy rains wash the minerals from the soil. When the soil becomes infertile, the farmers move on.

Over time, this type of farming, known as shifting cultivation, harms the environment. Many blame the Brazilian government for encouraging too many people to settle on land that is not really suitable for farming.

► As well as giving us chocolate, cocoa from the Amazon has been shown to reduce the risk of cancer, heart disease, and stroke.

Rain Forest Medicines

Plants that grow in the rain forest often have healing properties, and many plant remedies have been used by Amerindians for generations. The US National Cancer Institute has identified over 3,000 plants that help destroy cancer cells. Of these, around 75 percent are found in the Amazon rain forest.

The Várzea

YOU ARE HERE

From November to June each year, the Amazon is swollen by heavy rains, and land on either side of the river is flooded. The area affected by the flood is called the várzea, which means "flooded forest."

▼ The Amazon floodplain, known as the várzea, has some of the most fertile farmland in the Amazon basin.

Feeding the Floodplain

The Amazon flood is vital to the region. As the river spreads across the **floodplain**, it brings rich **sediment** called **silt** that turns the water a muddy brown. When the flood waters retreat, silt is left behind to **enrich** the soil. The rest of the silt is carried to the river's mouth, creating the **delta**.

◀ During the rainy season, forests in the várzea are flooded. Sometimes, trees are completely **submerged** and fish swim among the branches.

Farming the Floodplain

The people of the várzea use the river to help them farm the land. They build low banks of dirt that trap the floodwater and prevent it from draining back into the river. This water is used to **irrigate** crops during the dry season. The water sinks slowly into the soil, leaving silt that helps the crops to grow. This method is called "basin irrigation."

Harvesting Manioc

One of the most important crops grown in the várzea is manioc. When the manioc roots are big, farmers dig them up, peel them, and boil them to make a **pulp**. They squeeze the liquid out to get rid of poisons. The pulp is dried, then pounded into flour and used to make bread.

▶ A farmer and his family make farinha, a staple Brazilian food made from manioc roots.

Where Rivers Meet

BRAZIL

Rio Negro

Manaus

Amazon River

Purus River

Madeira River

YOU ARE HERE

South of Manaus, the Amazon is joined by its biggest tributary— the Rio Negro, or "black river." The point where the rivers meet is called their **confluence**.

The Rio Negro

The Rio Negro's source is 1,491 miles (2,400 km) northwest in the highlands of Colombia. Its dark color comes from the rotting leaves it picks up from the rain forest on its journey. The Amazon gets its milky color from the sediment it brings down from the Andes. For 50 miles (80 km), the two rivers flow side by side before finally merging.

▼ The Rio Negro bridge was built from 2008 to 2011. It connects Manaus and Iranduba.

◀ The lighter-colored waters of the Amazon meet the Rio Negro at Manaus.

Hydropower

The Amazon carries more water than any other river system on Earth. As well as helping to irrigate fields and grow crops, this water is used to generate electricity.

Since the 1970s, giant **hydroelectric** dams have been built on rivers throughout the Amazon basin. Supporters argue that the energy they supply is important for Brazil's economy, but many believe there are better ways to solve the country's energy needs. Because of fierce opposition from environmentalists and local people, many dam projects have recently been halted.

Victims of the Dams

Hydroelectric dams in the Amazon have wiped out plant and animal species, flooded **wetlands**, *and displaced thousands of people. Campaigners are now working with local communities and with Brazil's government to make sure that future projects safeguard the environment and respect the wishes of local people.*

▶ When large-scale dams are built, land behind the dam is flooded by the reservoirs. This often harms local communities.

21

Manaus

On the north bank of the Rio Negro is Manaus. This is the biggest city in the Amazon basin. It is home to 2 million people.

YOU ARE HERE

BRAZIL

Rio Negro

Manaus

Amazon River

Purus River

Madeira River

The Heart of the Amazon

Manaus started as a fort built by Portuguese settlers. Today, it is the region's most important commercial and industrial center. From here, ocean-going ships and cruise liners sail all the way to the river's mouth. Although it has an airport, Manaus is very isolated and has no rail links to other cities. The river is its most important link with the outside world.

▼ Amazon steamers unload goods and passengers at Manaus port.

◀ The Teatro Amazonica opera house in Manaus was built with money from the rubber trade.

Local Industries

Like Iquitos, Manaus became wealthy at the beginning of the last century from the trade in natural rubber. Steamboats carried the rubber downriver. From the coastal port of Belém, it was exported all over the world.

Today, rubber is still collected from the forest, but other industries are more important. Big cell phone companies such as Nokia have factories here. Oil is brought to the city to be turned into gasoline. Manaus is also a growing center for river cruises and ecotourism.

Ecotourism

Many visitors now come to see the scenery and wildlife of the Amazon basin. Ecotourists stay in simple wooden lodges in the rain forest and learn about the area with the help of local guides. Because numbers are limited, visitors can enjoy being close to nature without harming the environment.

▶ On ecotours, visitors can see the Amazon and its wildlife close up.

YOU ARE HERE

The Lower Amazon

As you travel the lower Amazon, you can see the dramatic changes that have taken place here. Huge areas of rain forest have been cleared to make way for large-scale farming and industry.

Roads, Logging, and Mining

In the past, plants, animals, and humans lived together here in a delicate balance. As trees have been cut down, plant and animal **habitats** have been lost, and the balance has been destroyed.

Since the 1980s, more than 6,200 miles (10,000 km) of new roads have been built through the Amazon rain forest. **Indigenous** people have been driven from their land by gangs of illegal loggers. Mining companies have moved in, and waste material from mines and industrial plants has drained into rivers and poisoned the fish.

◄ A new highway carves its way through what was once unspoiled rain forest.

◄ Many former forest areas are now occupied by cattle ranches. Beef from these ranches is sold to countries all over the world.

Protecting the Rain Forest

Today, the rate of deforestation is slowing. There are signs that the Brazilian government is finally acting to protect the rain forest.

Plans have been announced to divide the forest into zones and to limit cattle ranching to areas where wildlife is not endangered. New areas of forest will be planted, and mining and logging companies will have to plant trees on land that they have previously cleared. As the new forests grow, they will provide habitats for animals, and wildlife will gradually be encouraged to return to the area.

Tropical Hardwood

In the past, one of the main causes of deforestation was the cutting down of hardwood trees for export. Today, there are strict laws on the sale of hardwoods, and all timber must come from renewable sources. For every tree that is cut down, another has to be planted in its place.

► These **saplings** will be planted in areas of the Amazon that have been deforested.

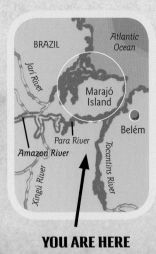

YOU ARE HERE

The Amazon Delta

As you approach the Amazon delta, the river splits into many channels that weave their way through islands of silt. These islands are constantly shifting as silt is built up and washed away by the flowing river.

Marajó Island

▼ During the rainy season, water buffalo grazing land on Marajó Island is flooded.

Marajó is the largest island in the delta. It covers an area the size of Switzerland. Two thousand years ago, it was occupied by Arua Indians. Today, the island is almost entirely populated by herds of water buffalo that graze in the marshy **pastureland**. According to local legend, the buffalo first arrived here after being shipwrecked in the delta.

▲ These wooded islands are made of silt dropped by the river.

Where River Meets Ocean

Beyond Marajó Island, the river finally reaches the ocean. But even here, its journey is not over. The current is so strong that it pushes the river hundreds of miles into the Atlantic, forming a plume of lighter-colored water. It was the sight of this river water so far out to sea that first led Spanish explorers to the Amazon 500 years ago.

▶ This Arua Indian vase was made some time between 1400 and 400 BC.

Clay from the River

The Arua Indians who once lived on Marajó Island were skilled potters. They used clay from the riverbank to make beautifully decorated vases, which they left to bake and harden in the sun. Potters on Marajó Island still make fine vases today.

Journey's End

At the city of Belém, the Amazon is joined by the Tocantins River. Here you reach the end of your Amazon adventure.

Belém was originally built as a fort by Portuguese settlers to defend their territory from other European invaders. It later became a center of the slave trade. Many of the people here are descended from slaves brought from Africa 300 years ago to work on plantations in the Amazon basin.

BRAZIL

Atlantic Ocean

Marajó Island

Belém

Para River

Tocantins River

Amazon River

YOU ARE HERE

▼ Cargo and ferry boats line the harbor at Belém. Behind is a market selling goods from all over the Amazon region.

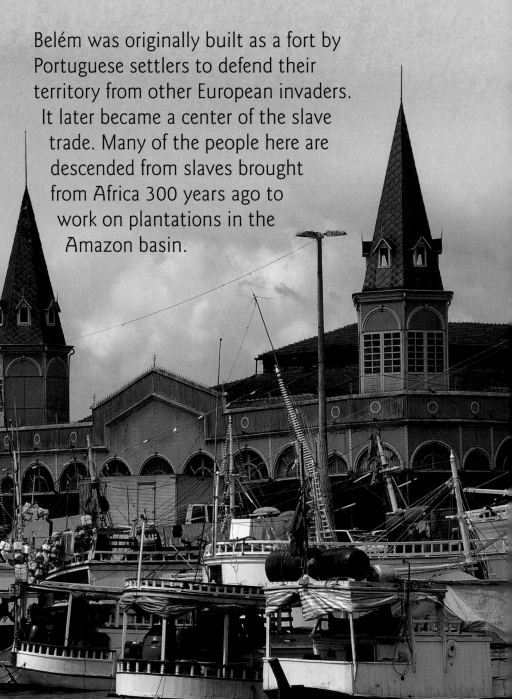

◀ An Amazon river steamer approaches the modern city of Belém.

A Busy Port

Because of its location at the river mouth, Belém was vital to the Portuguese traders. From here, ships would head across the Atlantic with cargos of spices, coffee, tobacco, and sugar. Other ships sailed upriver, bringing supplies to the settlements on the banks of the Amazon.

Today, more than 2 million people live in Belém, and all kinds of goods pass through its port. Timber is one of Brazil's biggest exports, and much of it is shipped abroad from Belém each year.

A Tasty Fruit

The tasty açaí fruit sold in Belém is a good example of an environmentally friendly crop. The fruit comes from a palm tree that grows on islands in the Amazon delta. The leaves of the palm are also used to make hats, mats, baskets, and **thatch** *for roofing.*

▶ A trader sells açaí fruit on the docks at Belém.

29

Glossary

blowgun a weapon made from a hollow tube that is used to shoot darts

canopy the top layer of foliage in a rain forest

confluence the point where two rivers meet

contaminated dirty or infected

delta the area at the mouth of a river where silt is deposited

dugout canoe a canoe made from the hollowed-out trunk of a tree

enrich to feed or nourish

estuary the place where a river widens and flows into the sea

floodplain the area affected by a river's floodwaters

habitat the natural home of a plant or animal

headwater the source of a river or stream

hydroelectric a type of electricity created from fast-flowing water

indigenous peoples the original inhabitants of a country or region

irrigate to bring water to a field in order to grow crops

logging cutting down trees for timber

meander a pattern of loops or bends formed by a river

natural resources materials that come directly from the natural environment

nutrient a source of food or nourishment

pastureland an area where cattle graze

plantation a large farm for growing a single crop

prehistoric before historic records began

pulp a mushy substance

sacred precious, holy

sapling a young tree

sediment broken down stones and mud from the riverbed

silt fine sediment carried downstream by a river

slave someone who is owned by another person and forced to work in cruel and inhumane conditions

species a type of plant or animal

stilt a length of timber used to raise a hut or house off the ground

submerge to swallow up or cover

subsistence farming growing just enough food to eat

terrace strips of level land cut into a hillside for farming

thatch a material used for covering a roof

tributary a river or stream that flows into another bigger one

wetland an area where the soil is waterlogged for all or part of the year

Amazon Quiz

Look up the information in this book or online. Find the answers on page 32.

1 Match the captions to the pictures.

1

2

3

4

5

6

A *A piranha fish*

B *Manioc roots*

C *An açaí palm*

D *An Amazon steamboat*

E *A heliconia plant*

F *A toucan*

2 These places can all be found along the Amazon. Place them in the right order, starting with the ones nearest to the sea:

Iquitos
Belém
Leticia
Manaus
Nauta
Santarém

4 This man is working by the banks of the Amazon. What is he doing?

3 True or false?

There are no bridges over the Amazon.

Websites and Further Reading

Websites

- *www.kids.nationalgeographic.com/ explore/countries/brazil/*
  A good, short introduction to Brazil.

- *www.rainforesteducation.com/medicines/ RFMedicines/medicines1.htm*
  An interesting short guide to plant medicines used by rain forest peoples.

- *gowild.wwf.org.uk/americas*
  Fact files, stories, games, and activities focusing on the Amazon rain forest.

Further Reading

Gibson, Karen. *The Amazon River* (Rivers of the World). Mitchell Lane Publishers, 2012.

Simon, Charnan. *They Mysterious Amazon* (Geography of the World). Child's World, Inc., 2014.

Woolf, Alex. *Journey Along the Amazon* (Traveling Wild). Gareth Stevens, 2014.

Index

Answers to Amazon Quiz
1 1D, 2C, 3A, 4E, 5F, 6B. **2** Belém, Santarém, Manaus, Leticia, Iquitos, Nauta. **3** True. The river mostly flows through tropical rain forest where there are very few roads or cities. There is therefore no need for crossings. **4** He is searching (panning) for gold in the riverbed.